Birds of the Northern Seas

Birds of the Northern Seas

by Ada and Frank Graham
Photographs by Les Line

DOUBLEDAY & COMPANY, INC.,
GARDEN CITY, NEW YORK

Library of Congress Cataloging in Publication Data
Graham, Ada.
Birds of the Northern Seas.
Includes index.
SUMMARY: Discusses the physical characteristics and behavior
of the large birds of the northern seas
including the auk, puffin, kittiwake,
storm petrel, gannet and others.
1. Sea birds—North Atlantic Ocean—Juvenile literature.
2. Sea birds—Juvenile literature.
3. Birds—North Atlantic Ocean—Juvenile literature.
[1. Sea birds. 2. Birds—North Atlantic Ocean]
I. Graham, Frank, 1925–   joint author.
II. Line, Les. III. Title.
QL676.2.G68   598.4'09163'1
Library of Congress Catalog Card Number 77–16916
ISBN: 0-385-12565-8 Trade
ISBN: 0-385-12566-6 Prebound

First Edition

The photographs on pages 6 and 7 were taken by Frank Graham.
The photograph on page 11 copyright ©
1979 Des and Jean Bartlett. BRUCE COLEMAN INC.
All other photographs were taken by Les Line.

Frontispiece photograph of gannets at nesting site.

Book design by Bente Hamann

Contents

1. The Island

DARKNESS CLOSED OVER THE ISLAND. A sliver of moon hung low in the sky, but clouds covered many of the stars. Waves crashed on the rocks at one end of the island, and bits of spray flashed like silver in the faint moonlight.

The island lay near the coast of Canada in the cold northern sea. A group of college students had come to the island in June to study the seabirds that nested there. The students lived in an old wooden building. All through the dark nights they could hear the waves rolling up onto the rocks and draining back into the sea.

At midnight one of the students got up and dressed. She put on low rubber boots and a warm jacket, because the nights were often damp and cold on the island, even in summer. She did not take a flashlight. She had been on the island for several weeks and she knew the path that went winding through the trees.

Soon she was in the midst of the forest that covered a part of the island. She walked slowly, trying not to stumble over the roots of the spruce trees. Through the feathery leaves of the mountain ash she glimpsed the moon, but its light didn't reach the floor of the forest, which was dark and murky.

She stopped and listened. The island seemed a lonely place at midnight. Surrounded by the forest, she could hardly hear the sound of the waves breaking on the shore. The gulls, which were so active by daylight, were now asleep or were silently guarding their nests. Someone who did not know the island would think that only the wind and the sea were stirring there at night.

But the student wasn't alone in the dark. A tiny form fluttered in front of her face and was gone in an instant. Another flew swiftly overhead, its dusky wings brightened for a moment in moonlight. The wings of another creature almost brushed her face as it dropped from the night sky and dove through an opening in the branches.

And all around her the forest seemed to ring with the soft, twittering voices of the swift little creatures. There was nothing scary about the voices. They rose out of the forest beside her, and then trailed away into nothingness, like the creatures themselves. She felt as if she were standing in a magical toy shop, where little music boxes suddenly burst into melody, one by one, and swiftly played themselves out. The sweet twitter made the forest seem enchanted. The student remembered that a scientist had once said that this song sounded as if it were made by elves or brownies.

But the student wasn't in an enchanted forest. She had come there to catch a glimpse of the living things she was trying to study. Each summer, this island forest was the home of a colony of storm petrels, dark little seabirds that come to dry land only to lay their eggs and raise their young. They were never seen about the island in daylight. They came and went only by night.

The student pushed her way through the branches at the edge of the path. The moonlight could not follow her there, but the birds' voices did. She stood with her back to a tree trunk and listened again. The twittering notes sounded through the branches as the birds came flying in from the sea. And in there among the trees there was another sound. It came straight up from the ground, from small openings in the forest floor, from between the roots of trees, and from under the cover of leaves. It was a soft, purring song. It came from many places under her feet, and it rose and fell in gentle rhythms, as if a tribe of musical cats were purring contentedly.

This was a sound that few human beings have heard. It was the song crooned by the storm petrels to their mates in the inky darkness of their burrows underground. The student stood there for a long time, listening to the mysterious birds. In the lonely darkness of the island it was easy to think of the storm petrels as creatures out of old fairy tales, like elves and brownies.

But daylight would soon come to the island again. Then it would be time to look more closely into these burrows and try to piece together the life story of one of the most extraordinary birds of the northern sea.

2. The Storm Petrel

IT WAS NATURAL TO CREATE MYTHS, or fanciful stories, about storm petrels. The sea was a place of danger and mystery for the early explorers and fishermen. They took comfort in any sign that God protected them and their ships. For many weeks at sea, the only living creatures they saw were storm petrels or close relatives of those birds.

Sailors told many stories about the dark birds they saw far at sea. The name of the birds—storm petrels—tells us that the sailors saw them as magical creatures. Some sailors said that the sight of these birds was a warning that a dangerous storm was coming.

As the birds followed a ship, searching for food, they seemed at times to be walking along the tops of the waves. Many people think that sailors called them petrels after Saint Peter, who is said to have walked on the waves with the help of Jesus. Sailors had never seen these birds on land, so they believed they spent their whole lives at sea. They said the storm petrel carried its egg under its wing and hatched it while flying over the ocean.

We know a great deal more about storm petrels today. Scientists have found their nesting places. We have a better idea of how they spend their time at sea. But there is much that we still don't know about storm petrels. Their lives are so strange to us that we can understand why the sailors of old believed there was something magical about them.

It was still early in the morning when the students began their work in the storm-petrel colony on Kent Island. Scientists who study birds are called ornithologists. For many years, ornithologists and their students have come to this island in the Bay of Fundy to try to find out more about these birds. The warm sun of late June was now over the sea. Thousands of gulls, which also nested on the island, were flying along the shore or sitting on the nests they had built high on the rocks.

A small group of students walked into the spruce forest, looking for new burrows of the storm petrels. It would be hard to find them without help. There are many holes in the floor of the forest among the roots of the trees and under large rocks. It would take a lot of time and patience to search all of those holes.

But the storm petrels themselves leave a clue. All members of this family of birds produce a thick, yellowish oil in their stomachs which they feed to their chicks. This oil has a strong musky odor, which lasts for a long time. Even the feathers of storm petrels that have been stored in museums for many years keep the odor of this oil.

The odor may be smelled easily near petrel burrows. The students who were looking for the burrows were able to "sniff them out," just as a dog sniffs out a rabbit hole. In this way they soon found a burrow under the roots of a spruce tree.

The students liked to say they were "grubbing for petrels." The word *grub* means to dig in the earth, just as archaeologists dig for bones. One of the petrel grubbers was named Liz. She had rolled up the right sleeve of her shirt, and her arm was already smudged with dirt from reaching into burrows.

Liz lay down on her side on the forest floor. She could smell the strong odor among the roots. She put her bare right arm into the hole. The soft, damp earth felt cool against her skin as she reached down the burrow, which ran straight for about two feet and then curved sharply. As she reached, Liz felt the burrow grow wider. She knew that her hand was in the nest chamber.

A student reaches into a petrel burrow in an island forest.

Now Liz grew very careful. She extended her fingers, feeling the loose earth on the chamber floor. Suddenly her fingers touched a soft, feathery object. The object struggled feebly to back away. Liz curled her fingers gently around it and pulled the bird out of the burrow. It was a storm petrel.

The bird sat quietly in Liz's hand, blinking in the sunlight. It did not try to escape. To Liz the little creature seemed to weigh no more than a handful of feathers—two ounces at most, or about fifty grams. The other petrel grubbers gathered around Liz for a closer look at the bird.

The seabird that she held is a species—or kind—called the Leach's storm petrel. It is named for a British scientist who lived in the nineteenth century. It was about eight inches long from the tip of its beak to the end of its forked tail, about the size of a blackbird. Its body was covered with brownish-black feathers across the wings and a clear white patch on its rump.

The student holds a small, dark petrel taken from its underground burrow.

The petrel's legs and tiny feet were shiny black, with webs between the toes. A storm petrel uses its legs mostly for swimming. They are too weak for the bird to stand on, so that when it tries to walk on dry land, it shuffles along on bent legs, partly pushing itself with its wings.

The most curious thing about the petrel was its short, black beak. Like all petrels, this bird had a pair of tubes set like small ridges on top of its beak. A petrel's nostrils are contained in these tubes.

Tube nostrils are found only on birds that produce oil in their stomachs. Scientists believe that the birds use this oil in preening —or dressing—their feathers. It is important for a bird that lives at sea to keep its dense coat of feathers trim and neat. Petrels release oil through their nostrils onto their feathers while waterproofing them with the beak.

Because they spend their lives at sea, storm petrels find only salt water to drink. Glands in their heads remove the excess salt from the water. Then the salt escapes through the tube nostrils.

Liz handed the bird to another student and reached into the burrow again. This time she drew out an egg. Most land birds lay two or more eggs when they nest, but storm petrels and many other seabirds lay only one. Often they must fly long distances to find food, and it would be difficult to feed more than a single chick. The petrel's oval egg was about an inch and a quarter long. Its white shell was smooth but not shiny, and there were faint reddish spots at one end.

Liz put the egg back in the burrow. Then, holding the storm petrel carefully, she banded it. She used a light, aluminum band, which she slipped over the bird's dainty foot and closed with a small pair of pliers. In her notebook she wrote down the number that was stamped on the band and the exact location of the burrow on the island. In future years other scientists who found this bird would be able to check the number on the band and learn something about its movements from year to year.

There was one thing Liz could not tell about this bird. She did not know whether it was a male or a female, because all adult storm petrels look exactly alike and both sexes will brood the egg. Only by dissecting a dead petrel can a scientist tell its sex.

Liz smoothed the little bird's ruffled feathers back into place and put it into its burrow. She held her hand over the opening for a moment in case the bird became confused or panicky and tried to fly out. In that case the gulls would quickly overtake it in its fluttery flight and kill it. That is why the storm petrels come and go on the island only at night.

6. The Cliff

MUCH OF WHAT THE WORLD KNOWS about the Leach's storm petrel was learned there on Kent Island. By numbering and keeping a record of each burrow and banding the birds found in them, the ornithologists and their students have uncovered some of their secrets.

They learned that some of the storm petrels live to a ripe old age. One of the petrels had only one foot, and the students called it "Long John Silver," after the peg-legged pirate. "Long John" returned to Kent Island every summer, and its band revealed that it was more than twenty-five years old.

Another storm petrel was banded as a chick on the island. Four years later, it returned to the island to dig a burrow less than four feet away from that of its parents. Several years later, the scientists found it back in the burrow where they had banded it as a chick. Now it was raising a chick of its own.

For most of the year, the Leach's storm petrel is a bird of the northern oceans. It nests on islands in the North Pacific and on both sides of the Atlantic Ocean. No one is quite sure where these birds spend the winter, but it is somewhere far at sea. Many of them probably fly to the South Atlantic.

They begin to arrive at Kent Island in May. Often they return to the same burrows with the same mates year after year. If the storm petrels have not had a burrow before, or if the old burrow has collapsed, the male digs a new one. A naturalist who watched the petrels has described how they do it:

"In the construction of the burrow the bird used both its bill and feet. The bill serves as a sort of pick to loosen up the dirt. The sharp toenails scrape the dirt aside and the soles of the feet pat it down. Little soil is actually removed from the mouth of the burrow. The ground is loosely packed on the island, and the birds need only to press the earth into a compact mass on the floor of the burrow."

It takes the male three days to dig the burrow. On Kent Island the birds do not build a true nest inside the burrow, but lay the egg on the bare ground. On other islands Leach's storm petrels often line the nest chamber with small twigs, dried grass, or feathers. Sometimes sheep are kept on the islands where these birds nest, and then they may use sheep's wool.

Storm petrels mate in the burrow on the night it is finished. The following night, the female lays the egg. For the next forty-two days the parent birds take turns incubating the egg while the other flies out to sea in search of the squid and other small creatures on which it feeds.

On many islands this is a dangerous time for storm petrels. Rats, or cats and dogs brought to an island by human beings, may get into the burrows and kill the birds or destroy the eggs. Many years ago, the lighthouse keeper on an island off the coast of Maine kept a Newfoundland dog. A scientist visited the island and found that the dog spent much of its time digging the petrels out of their burrows.

"Apparently he did this purely for the sport of it, for we found the bodies of the petrels lying where he had killed them," the scientist wrote. "Perhaps the strong-smelling oily fluid which the birds ejected prevented his eating them, but did not discourage his digging out and killing them. After a few years this large colony was practically destroyed."

When the chick hatches, its eyes are closed and it is helpless. For a few days the adults feed the chick on the yellow oil they

Adult Wilson's storm petrel. Photo by Des and Jen Bartlett.

bring up from their stomachs. One of the parents stays with the chick day and night. The helpless creature spends most of its time stretched on the floor of the burrow, the tip of its bill resting on the ground, dozing or lying quietly. Sometimes it utters a feeble *queak*.

Soon the parents leave the chick by itself during the day while they go out to sea to hunt for food. But at night the island comes alive as the storm petrels return to tend their eggs or feed their chicks. Fluttering and swooping like bats, the birds fly into the forest and enter their burrows among the roots of trees.

How does a storm petrel find its own nest in the dense forest after dark? Most kinds of birds have very little sense of smell, but scientists have found that tube-nosed birds like the storm petrels seem to have a keen sense of smell. They believe that these birds are able to recognize the special musky odor that clings to their own burrows.

The chick grows quickly in the burrow. Its eyes open. Dark feathers begin to push out through the soft fluff that covers its body from the first days of its life. It grows fat, like a little butterball, and after about six weeks it weighs nearly twice as much as its parents!

The chick remains in the burrow for about ten weeks. Summer fades into autumn. The nights on the island grow cold. The parent birds come to the burrow only seldom now. The chick lives mainly on the large amount of oily fat it has stored in its own body. It begins to lose weight, and soon weighs no more than an adult storm petrel. The parent birds leave the island to fly toward their winter feeding grounds and the chick is left alone.

On warm days, the chick crawls from the burrow on its weak little legs and sits in the sun. It exercises its long, dusky wings to get the feel of flight. It cannot remain in the burrow much longer. The storms of winter are on the way and they will clog the burrow's opening with ice.

On a dark night at the end of October, the chick begins to sense the call of the sea. It makes its way out of the burrow, but it has trouble getting into the air. Flapping its wings with great energy, it struggles onto a low mound of earth. Then, half tumbling from the mound and with its wings flapping harder still, it finds itself in the air and flies swiftly and easily out over the dark ocean.

Dawn comes late to this northern island. Now the island belongs to the creatures of the daylight—mostly a few gulls that nest there during the summer and remain for a while to feed on its rocky shore.

4. The Sea

To SOME PEOPLE the North Atlantic is a vast, empty surface, like the face of the moon. They see it simply as a boring stretch of water and sky that exists between the continents of Europe and North America. But other people have looked at the ocean more closely. They see it as a great stage where some of the world's most remarkable living things act out the drama of their lives against a background of white-topped waves, thick fogs and fierce storms.

Imagine you are standing on the bow of a ship that has left land behind. The North Atlantic stretches away on all sides as far as the eye can see. In the distance, sea and sky meet at the horizon so that the ship seems to be closed under a giant bowl. And now, if you look closely, you will see that you are not alone.

Flying back and forth in the ship's wake are three or four small dark birds. They are Wilson's storm petrels. They look much like the Leach's storm petrels that Liz and the others studied on Kent Island. But an expert can tell them apart because this bird has shorter, more rounded wings and a more fluttery flight. Its legs, which are longer than the Leach's petrel's, extend beyond the tip of the tail.

But there is an unseen difference, too. The Wilson's storm petrels nest many thousands of miles away. They dig their burrows and raise their young on islands in the far south, between the tip of South America and the Antarctic Ocean. Their chicks hatch in February, which is the middle of summer in the southern hemisphere.

By April, millions of these birds fly up across the equator and into the North Atlantic. They follow the warm weather north. Some scientists believe that the Wilson's storm petrel is the most numerous bird in the world. These are the storm petrels that sailors usually see on the ocean. They fly just over the water, looking for small sea creatures or scraps thrown from ships. As they search, their long legs keep patting the water as though they were dancing across the waves.

Hundreds of years ago, English sailors who noticed these little birds called them "Mother Carey's chickens." This was the way they pronounced Mater Cara, which are Latin words that mean "Dear Mother," or the Mother of God. The sailors believed that the storm petrels, which seemed to appear out of nowhere on the great empty sea, were a sign that heaven protected them.

But Mother Carey's chickens do not appear out of nowhere. Aside from the time they spend on their nesting islands, they live out their lives on the sea. They live in a harsh world, as all seabirds do. There is no shelter for them on the open sea. There are no burrows or bushes in which they can hide from the cold rain and tearing wind. Sometimes after great storms thousands of seabirds are washed up dead or dying on beaches. These little feathered creatures, which weigh only a few ounces, must fight for their lives all year long in gales and mighty waves.

The Current of Life

The stage of this drama is the North Atlantic Ocean. Its boundary is a huge circle that begins along the sandy beaches of the eastern United States and curves up past the rocky coast of Maine. It touches eastern Canada at Nova Scotia.

Then the sweep of the circle travels north and eastward past the great islands that mark the approaches to the Arctic: Newfoundland, Greenland and Iceland. More than three thousand miles east of where it began, our imaginary line reaches the British Isles. It follows the coast of western Europe to the south, and finally returns across the sea to the United States.

We have said that life can be hard for birds in the North Atlantic. But millions of birds spend their lives there, or come to it for a part of the year. It must offer some rewards to attract so many birds. You might say that this cold ocean offers birds a good living.

The secret of the North Atlantic is that it *moves*. It is a world where something is always happening. The ocean is alive with currents. Currents are to the water very much like what the winds are to the air. They are always moving, and they bring change wherever they go.

A current is a flow of water moving through the quiet sea around it. The current that changes the North Atlantic begins its journey far to the south. It forms on the equator near the coast of Africa. The wind that comes off the African continent disturbs the warm water on the ocean's surface. It blows this water farther away from the shore.

Beneath this layer of warm water lies a mass of cold water. It rises to the surface to replace the warm water that the winds have driven away. As the cold water rises, it brings with it nourishing minerals from the deep. Tiny plants called phytoplankton live near the surface of the water. Now, turning these minerals into nourishment with the aid of the bright southern sunlight, the plants grow and multiply.

This area of the ocean is very rich in life. Tiny sea animals called zooplankton, which drift on the surface of the water, feed on the tiny plants. They grow and multiply too. Other sea animals, such as small squids and shrimp, gather to feed on the zooplankton. Finally, larger fish and seabirds come to eat the smaller animals.

Wind and water, constantly moving, have created an enormous

food chain. The tiny plants thrive in this area. They become food for tiny animals that also exist there in great numbers. Larger and larger animals gather there, feeding on smaller ones. It is a place of movement and life.

Life is not found in such numbers in all parts of the ocean. In some places there is little movement and no swell of nourishing minerals from below. Scientists call these places "deserts of the ocean," because very few living things are found there. No rich currents flow in or out of those regions.

As our planet, earth, turns on its axis, the surface moves from west to east. At the equator, this movement of the earth acts strongly on both air and water. These two elements, air and water, respond to the earth's turning by moving in the opposite direction. They flow westward as winds and currents.

The rich water off the coast of Africa is carried northwestward across the ocean as a strong current. Near the Gulf of Mexico it picks up new nutrients, and some warmer water as well. It flows up the coast of North America on a great circle, ending where it began. For a time, this warmer current is called the Gulf Stream. It crosses the ocean and washes the shores of the British Isles.

Other currents form in the icy regions of the Arctic. They flow south along the coast of Greenland and North America. Wherever these currents meet, there is a great disturbance in the water. Storms create further turbulence. Cold water mingles with warmer water. In the water's agitation, the nourishing minerals are carried to the surface. Another food chain is created.

There are a number of places in the North Atlantic where the moving water creates these enormous centers of life. Among these places are the Grand Banks, off Newfoundland, and the productive fishing regions near the British Isles. The people of southern Europe have known about these fishing grounds for hundreds of years. Fishing boats from Portugal and other European countries were crossing the Atlantic regularly at the time of Columbus.

The promise of fish of all sizes has attracted millions of birds to the North Atlantic too. Some birds, such as Wilson's storm petrels, fly all the way from Antarctic regions to spend the summer months on these fishing grounds. Many other kinds of birds spend all of their lives in the North Atlantic.

And so, as you stand on the bow of a boat in the North Atlantic, you know that there is no empty "desert" around you.

Life on the Sea

Birds evolved as creatures of the land. Even today, by far the largest share of the world's 8,600 kinds of birds live on land. Only 285 kinds are seabirds. But most of the birds that have adopted the life of the sea have done very well, and until recent years numbered in the millions.

Nature has fitted these birds well for life in the harsh climate of the northern sea. The body of each kind of bird has become adapted to a rough, cold, watery environment. When we look at a seabird trying to walk on land, we believe it is very clumsy. But that's because it seldom needs its legs for walking.

Some seabirds, such as storm petrels, find their food by flying over the water. Often they must fly a long distance in search of food. Their wings are quite long in proportion to their bodies, so they may fly easily. Their legs are small and weak, which allows their light bodies to move more easily through the air.

Other seabirds, such as murres and puffins, find their food by swimming underwater. Their wings are short and stubby and can be used as flippers. Their stout legs are set far back on their bodies, which helps to push them through the water. The position of their legs makes them strong swimmers but clumsy walkers.

The sea must provide birds with other things besides food. It must give them places to nest. Birds cannot lay their eggs in the air or on the open water, as the sailors in old times thought storm petrels did.

Yet it is difficult for seabirds to nest on the mainland or on the larger islands. Those places are the homes of many other kinds of animals: raccoons, rats, foxes, dogs, and cats. Seabirds, because they are fitted for life at sea, are too clumsy to escape those animals on land. We have seen that a single dog nearly destroyed a colony of storm petrels when it was brought to an island where they nested.

But the sea is not simply an empty stretch of water. It throws up sandbars where terns and gulls may nest. Scattered around the edge of the sea are small islands, covered with trees or grasses, that cannot be reached by foxes and raccoons unless human beings bring them there. Giant rocks called stacks, which are often the tops of undersea mountains, rise out of the ocean too. Seabirds find places to nest on all of these sandbars, islands, and stacks.

If you are ever on a ship at sea, keep watching for the birds around you. Gulls fly behind the ship, looking for scraps from its kitchen. Storm petrels, or Mother Carey's chickens, dance lightly over the waves. A tern circles overhead, then folds its wings and plunges into the water to capture a slender, silvery fish.

Far off, on the horizon, an island rises darkly out of the sea. There seems to be a shimmering cloud over the island. But as the ship draws close to it, you see that the cloud is made up of thousands of living things. Coming closer still, you see that each of those living things is a seabird. Each one is carrying food back to its nest on the island, or hurrying out to sea in its endless search for food.

Life on the northern ocean goes on, day and night.

5. Wings

IT IS EASY TO TELL A BIRD FROM ALL OTHER LIVING THINGS. Just see if it has feathers. If an animal has feathers, it is a bird. If it doesn't have feathers, it is not a bird. The matter is as simple as that.

Yet when we see a bird, we are most likely to think of its ability to fly. Bees, butterflies and bats can fly too, and even flying fish! But birds generally seem to us to be the most marvelous fliers of all.

One of the most beautiful sights in the world is a gull circling in a bright blue sky. The wings grow dazzling white as the sun shines on them. The gull seems to attract all the light in the sky to show off its airborne body.

A gull's wing is like a fine instrument. It is powerful, lifting a standing gull almost instantly into the air. Beating about twice each second, it sends the gull swiftly through the air in search of food or away from its enemies.

A gull's wing is very agile, too. It is able to take advantage of every puff of wind, tilting one way or the other so that the gull can glide or soar for long distances. This is an important advantage on the sea, where there are few resting places for birds. A gull is able to ride the winds without flapping its outstretched wings, just as you can coast downhill on a bicycle without pushing the pedals.

The strong wings of birds have taken them to places where other animals cannot go. A rugged mountain, a harsh desert, or a dense jungle may stop most animals. A bird simply flies over them. Even before human beings had boats, birds were able to reach the loneliest islands in the middle of the ocean.

Wings carry a bird to its feeding grounds or its nesting place. Wings are also a bird's best defense. When it meets an enemy, a bird does not have to stand and fight. It just flies away.

Seabirds have found a special use for their wings. Most of the food to be found at sea is provided by fish or other sea creatures that live underwater. Some seabirds have learned to use their wings like the fins of a fish or the flippers of a seal. They have learned to swim with their wings.

The auks are good underwater swimmers. They are a family of seabirds that include puffins, murres, and razorbills. All the auks feed by diving beneath the water's surface and swimming after little fish. An ornithologist who watched razorbills swimming underwater has told us how they do it:

"The wings are moved together—flapped or beaten—so that the bird really flies through the water. In flight, they are spread straight without a bend in them, but in the water they are bent at the joint. The wings are raised and brought down again toward the sides in the same position in which they rest against the sides when closed. The razorbill can dive to great depths, swim for long distances, and remain on the water for a long time."

The most curious member of this family of birds was the great auk. This seabird became so skillful at catching fish underwater that it no longer needed to fly. It spent all its time on the water along those currents where the fish appeared in large numbers. It used its wings only as flippers. Finally, the great auk lost the ability to fly.

Down through the ages, the great auk found a good life in the North Atlantic. It was a powerful swimmer and was able to catch all the fish it needed. When it came time to nest, it pulled

A gull can soar for long distances on air currents.

itself out of the water onto the low rocks of an island, just like a seal or a walrus. It had few enemies in the northern ocean.

Life changed quickly for the great auk when human beings began to build sturdy oceangoing boats. Once, these birds had nested on many of the small islands off North America and northern Europe. Then, fishermen began to visit those distant islands. During the nesting season, they saw the auks—large black-and-white birds, about the size of a goose, with round white spots on their faces.

The fishermen at first called these birds "penguins," which means "white head" in the Welsh language. Many years later, when the whaling boats reached the seas in the southern hemisphere, they found other birds that were not able to fly. They called them "penguins" too, and that name has stayed with the southern birds.

This was the beginning of a time when great numbers of seabirds were killed. Sailors learned to visit the islands during the nesting season. They killed the seabirds for food, or to use as bait when they were fishing. They also collected their eggs as food.

There was a big difference in the fate of the penguins in the southern sea and the great auks in the northern sea. Penguins often nested on islands close to Antarctica. These islands were hard to reach, so many penguins escaped the sailors who came to kill them. But the great auks nested on islands off Europe and North America, which were not so difficult to reach. On one island after another, the sailors slaughtered the great auks.

By the year 1800, there were very few great auks left alive. It was not worthwhile hunting them for food or bait anymore. Some people, however, paid hunters to kill these rare birds so that they could have them stuffed and mounted in museums and private collections at home.

There were no great auks left on the islands off North America. Two of them nested in the Orkney Islands, north of Scotland, in 1812. The people there called them the King and Queen of the Auks. But a hunter came to the island and killed both of them.

By 1840 these birds were almost extinct in the British Isles, too. Two men who found one on an island that year had no idea what it was. They killed it because they thought it was a witch. Four years later, a party of hunters went ashore on the island of Eldey, near Iceland. They found two great auks and beat them to death with clubs. They brought the skins back to a man who stuffed birds. No one ever saw a great auk alive again.

The great auk had become skillful at catching fish. But in becoming a powerful swimmer it had lost the ability to fly. It could no longer escape from its enemy, man. Fortunately, the other seabirds of the northern ocean have kept the power of flight. Beating against a stiff wind in a storm, or soaring high in a cloudless sky, the seabirds remain to add beauty and excitement to this part of the world.

3. The Chick

ALL OVER THE EDGES of the North Atlantic, great rocky islands rise out of the water. Sometimes the shore of these islands slopes gently down to the water. But very often the shore is simply a wall that is several hundred feet high.

An island cliff of the northern ocean is not a smooth surface. It is open to the raging storms. The huge slab of rock has been chipped and cracked. Water from rain and waves drips into the cracks, freezes during the winter, and splits the rock still further. The wind and the waves wear down other parts of the cliff. Pieces of rock break off and lie near the top of the island or on the shore below.

The face of a cliff is sculptured by storms and waves. The cracks grow wide and deep to form crevices. Storm-driven seas burst into these crevices and hollow them out. Narrow ledges are carved by nature into broad platforms. On some islands, grasses and shrubs grow a bright green. Old-time sailors used to wonder about these natural gardens until they realized that they were fertilized every year by the droppings from birds that nested on the cliffs above them.

Many of these cliffs in the northern sea are tall apartment houses for seabirds. There are few places the same size in all the world that hold as many vertebrate animals—those that have

Great, rocky islands of the North Atlantic provide nesting sites for thousands of seabirds.

backbones—as an ocean cliff. Thousands of birds may build their nests there in the spring. A visitor to the cliffs sees birds standing at every crevice and crowded on every ledge. Other birds stream past the cliff like snowflakes in a blizzard.

Yet the birds on the cliff are not scattered about by accident. Each kind of seabird prefers a different place on which to build its nest. Each one prefers a different "room" in this giant apartment house.

The larger gulls usually take the places on level ground on top of the cliff. From there they can watch the birds below them and fly down to seize an egg or a chick in a nest that is left unguarded. Gannets, which are larger seabirds, build their nests up there too, or on the widest ledges in the cliff.

Small gulls called kittiwakes choose narrow ledges. Razorbills like protected ledges or crevices. Their hardy relatives, the murres (rhymes with *purrs*), prefer more exposed ledges. Still other birds, the black guillemots (gill-uh-mots), nest under the boulders that have tumbled near the shore below.

Most of us can think of many more comfortable places to build a nest. Rain and winds sweep the face of the cliff. The ledges are usually narrow, and there are heaps of jagged boulders on the shore below. But seabirds are tough. They have learned to live in the worst kinds of weather. On the cliff, the seabirds, their eggs, and their young are safe from most predators. Only gulls, falcons, and a few other predatory birds can reach their high nests.

Even human beings find it hard to reach these nests. One of America's most famous ornithologists, whose name was Arthur C. Bent, wrote a description of his visit to the tall cliffs of Bird Rock, a Canadian island, in 1904. Bent came to the island at night when the sea was very rough. This is what he wrote:

"As the great cliffs towered above us in the moonlight we saw a lantern coming down the ladder to show us where to land. We ran the boat in among the breaking waves. There was a crash which brought us to our feet as we struck an unseen rock. But the next wave carried us over it and landed us among the rocks and flying spray.

"We were overboard in an instant, struggling in the surf up to our waists, for the boat was rapidly filling, as wave after wave broke over us. After exchanging greetings with the keeper of the lighthouse on the island we enjoyed the special experience of being hoisted up in a crate to the top of the cliff 100 feet high.

"It was certainly a new and interesting sensation to feel ourselves slowly rising in the darkness up the face of those cliffs. The surf was thundering on the rocks below us. A cloud of screaming seabirds was flying around us. We could barely see them in the moonlight. The seabirds were like a swarm of ghostly bats whose sleep had been disturbed and who were protesting at our rude coming."

The next day, Bent climbed back into the wooden crate. Then the lighthouse keepers lowered him on a long rope partway down the face of the cliff. There he hung in the crate as it twisted in the wind, only a few feet away from the birds that nested on the ledges.

Bent made notes about what he saw at the cliff. He even managed to take photographs of the birds and their nests. He was willing to experience danger and many uncomfortable moments so that he could study seabirds on the cliff.

Seabirds nest on cliffs because they feel safe from their enemies there, yet they must develop a way of life that fits them to survive. Each kind of bird finds ways to raise its young safely in this dangerous world.

7. Learning to Be a Parent

A FEVERISH EXCITEMENT is the mood that ran through all the birds on the cliff in spring. Gulls, murres, razorbills, gannets and puffins were returning from their winter at sea. Many of the birds approached the cliff carefully. They circled it on rapidly beating wings or floated lightly among the waves offshore. Some of the birds had already landed on the rocks.

A change was coming over the birds. Each one had fought for its existence during the winter. It had caught fish and ridden out the storms because it had learned how to take care of itself. All winter long, a seabird could not depend on help from any other living creature. It kept its distance from the other birds. It may have traveled in a flock, but each bird was on its own.

A seabird, as it drifted in the surf near the cliff, had the means to defend itself. If it hadn't, it would have died long before. As a chick, it had learned the laws of its wild world. The bird knew when to give in to a stronger bird and retreat. It found that there were other birds that it could bully too.

When food was scarce, as it sometimes was in the winter, a bird had to fight for its share. The weak ones starved. A seabird lived by being strong. It lived by defending itself against other birds.

A gannet lands at a crowded nesting site on a cliff.

Now the gannets, the murres, and the other birds had to make an amazing change in their way of life. They had kept their distance from other birds. They did not really trust even the birds in their own flock. But the time had come to mate and raise their young. Each bird had to overcome its distrust of the others and settle down peacefully with a mate.

First, many of the birds had to overcome their fear of the land. Puffins, murres, and razorbills flew over the island in flocks. They landed and investigated the rocks. Then they grew uneasy and flew back to sea.

The birds that swam in the surf seemed to be at play. The razorbills and puffins floated high on the surface and could be told at a distance from the murres, whose backs were sometimes nearly under the water. There was a great deal of splashing and diving. Whole flocks of murres suddenly dove beneath the waves. A watcher on the cliff would see the birds slowly moving their wings underwater, pushing themselves lazily along, and steering with their big, webbed feet.

There were frequent chases on the surface of the water. A bird would dart at another one, so that the other would scurry off in fright. The razorbills and murres seemed to take special delight in chasing the puffins, which are smaller birds. Sometimes a bird would sneak up underwater on a puffin and nip its tail. The surprised puffin would nearly leap out of the water.

Yet all of this diving and splashing was not done purely in fun. The seabirds were preparing for some very serious business. For many long months, they had survived by being on the defensive with all other creatures. Now the nesting time was near. They had to get rid of their fears. They had to choose a mate and learn to live peacefully with that bird so that they could raise a healthy chick.

The birds on the water were beginning to break down the barriers between them. Birds approached each other, but their feelings were still all mixed up. A razorbill swam up to another one and tried to rub beaks with it. The other bird flew swiftly away or, sometimes, turned and fought. There were lots of little squabbles on the water.

A flock of puffins perch on a rocky cliff.

The razor-bill auk is a handsome black-and-white bird that resembles the extinct auk.

The beaks or bills of the birds became very important. The puffin's beak, which had been very drab in winter, suddenly blossomed like a flower. It was colored with blue and bright red. The bird threatened other puffins with its stout beak, or tried to rub it against theirs.

The beaks of the other members of the auk family were dark and not so prominent. They called attention to their beaks by opening them. When a razorbill opened its beak, the lining was bright yellow. A murre's beak lining was also yellow, while the smaller black guillemot flashed a scarlet lining.

The seabirds around the cliff were taking part in that important activity that scientists call *display*. They were beginning to court their mates for the nesting season. They were using the bright colors of their beaks to attract a member of the opposite sex, just as human beings use their best clothes or a fancy hairdo.

In most kinds of land birds, the male does most of the display. He has brightly colored feathers or a long, streaming tail or a fancy-colored comb or wattles, as some of the chickenlike birds do. The male performs complicated dances in front of the female of his choice. He goes to great lengths to win her. But once he does win her, the female does most of the work: building a nest, incubating the eggs, and feeding the chicks.

Ornithologists say that seabirds make "model husbands." The males do not have the advantage of brighter plumage. Both sexes look almost exactly the same. They both take part in the display. Later the males share with the females the duties of building the nest and caring for the eggs and chicks.

When birds display, they are sending signals. One of the difficulties of being a seabird is that males and females usually look so much alike that even *they* cannot tell one from the other at first sight. Display helps to solve the problem. As we shall see, a seabird uses its beak to pass on signals.

Signals

Seabirds, when they arrive at the cliff, are still confused. They don't know whether they want to attack another bird or mate with it. They are still suspicious of all the other birds. At the start of the nesting season, the birds generally use their beaks as weapons.

A puffin that has just arrived at the cliff meets another puffin. Over a span of many centuries, these birds have worked out a series of signals. The puffin that advances toward another one with its beak held down and its feathers ruffled up is behaving in a threatening way. A man who walks toward another person with his fists clenched and a scowl on his face is also behaving in a threatening way. Both the puffin and the man are looking for trouble.

In the case of the male puffin, this signal may be valuable at nesting time. If the puffin he approaches either fights back or flies away, he knows that bird is another male. A female puffin often behaves differently in response to the threat. She will turn her beak aside to show that she is not offering a threat of her own. She wants to be friends with this fierce-looking male. She may want to become his mate. The male puffin knows he has found a female.

These signals do not always work. Many young birds who have never nested before come to the cliff in the spring. They are not always sure how the signals work. They may be confused, or hesitate to display. These birds probably will not find a mate that year.

The female seabird has been attracted to the male by his display. She has shown him she wants to be friends. Now the two birds must make the bond firm between them if they are to mate successfully. They touch each other's beak and do much bowing and scraping. By repeating these courtship dances, both on water and on land, seabirds break down the barriers of distrust. They make a bond between them.

The two birds, male and female, then mark out a territory for themselves. There is very little room on the cliff. The nesting birds are crowded together on the ledges and in the crevices. The older birds, which are more experienced and often stronger than the others, take the best nesting places, at the center of the colony. The younger birds must fight for places at the edge of the colony or on the ends of the ledges.

Safety in Numbers

Ornithologists have noticed a curious fact about seabird colonies. The birds seem to prefer being crowded. At some colonies the birds barely have room to walk around their nests. Birds flying back to their nests cannot find room to land, and they crash into their neighbors. Yet even when a colony has been struck by a disaster and there is plenty of room on the ledges, the birds still crowd together at the center.

Why do these seabirds—the gannets, the auks, the terns, and the gulls—nest so closely packed? Ornithologists who have care-

Gannets, like many other seabirds, feel secure when they nest in crowded, noisy colonies.

A gannet begins its display, or courtship behavior.

fully watched the nesting colonies have found that seabirds nest more successfully in dense crowds. They are more likely to raise their chicks that way than if they looked for nests that were at some distance from the others.

The cliffs and islands where seabirds nest have very few places to hide nests. Trees and thick shrubs cannot grow where they are attacked every winter by gale winds and huge waves. Some of the seabirds, such as puffins and storm petrels, nest in burrows. But most of the birds must nest on the open ledges and slopes.

Seabirds that nest in these open places are more successful if they raise their young quickly. There is less chance of a disaster. The birds that are crowded together on the cliff tend to copy their neighbors. The older birds, being more experienced, usually

In a greeting ceremony, the gannet rubs beaks with its mate.

Bowing and nodding are also part of the ceremony.

One gannet may rest its head upon the other.

go right to work and then begin nesting. Other birds, only a few feet away, are stimulated to begin nesting too. By showing the way, the older birds set the tone. The whole colony nests at about the same time. The chicks are more likely to grow and leave the colony before the storms of late summer.

There is safety in numbers too. When predators fly over the colony, they may not be as likely to try to invade such a dense mass of birds. They will generally raid the nests of the younger birds that are scattered on the edge of the colony.

Excitement and noise remain the rule on the cliff all summer. Seabirds do not stop their display once they have found a mate and the egg is laid. All through the nesting season, the excitement runs high as both parents tend the nest. They bow and nod, they rub their beaks together, they keep the courtship going. The bond between them must be kept firm so that both birds share in the work of raising a chick.

Every act at the nest strengthens the bond between the parents. The chick learns to recognize its parents. It, too, becomes part of the family bond. The knowledge that its parents are not a threat to it will help it to recognize other birds of its kind when it comes time for it to find a mate of its own.

The display between parents continues until they have finished their job. The ceremonies at the nest have helped the parent birds to overcome the feelings that guide them for most of the year. In late summer, the bowing and the beak-rubbing come to an end. The chick no longer needs its parents. The remarkable bond is broken.

Let's take a closer look at how the bond between seabirds works to help a particular species.

8. Life on a Ledge

A MAN AND A WOMAN sat in the damp grass, shielded from the wind by the big rock beside them. They were ornithologists and had come to watch the cliff across the cove. Birds of many kinds flew up to the cliff from the sea. The waves that hurled themselves on the shore exploded in clouds of spray hundreds of feet below.

The island, with its tall cliff, lay in the sea many miles off the coast of England. Still, the noise around the man and woman seemed to be as loud as if they were on a busy street in a great city. The crashing of the waves sounded like thunder. The birds massed on the ledges were never quiet. They cooed and grunted and groaned and shrieked.

The man and the woman, like Arthur Bent many years before them, were studying seabirds. They did not have to hang from a rope in a crate to get a good view of the birds. They brought modern, high-powered binoculars and telescopes to see what was going on at the cliff.

Watching seabirds is not always easy even today. The watchers must travel by small boat to islands far from the mainland. In bad weather it is dangerous to land, because the waves pound the boat against the rocks on the island shore. The shore itself is slippery with dripping seaweed. There is little protection against wind and rain on these barren islands. For days at a time, the islands may be draped in fog or drenched in cold rain.

The watchers must have great patience. They must sit quietly for many hours. Often, very little seems to be going on in front of them. The birds act in a way that sometimes does not seem to make much sense. But the watchers write down in their notebooks every movement they see. They know that every detail is important, like the letters in a code. They are trying to solve the code of a seabird's life.

After days, or even years, of watching, ornithologists find that the movements finally begin to make some sense. Little by little, piece by piece, the watchers patiently put together the true story of what it is like to be a seabird.

The man and the woman were watching the murres on the cliff. In Great Britain these birds are called common guillemots. They are members of the family of auks and are closely related to the puffins and razorbills as well as to the great auk. The feathers on their head, neck, back, and wings are brownish black, but their undersides are pure white. The black bill is slender and pointed.

The murres were packed onto the ledges like ranks of soldiers. On one of the larger ledges there were eight rows of murres, with about twenty-five birds in each row. Many of the birds stood with their backs to the sea, staring into the cliff wall.

Other murres were sitting on their eggs. Murres do not build a nest of any kind. A female simply lays her large, pale egg covered with dark blotches on the bare rock. The egg has to have a tough shell, because it is treated roughly on the ledge. It is shaped like a pear, with one end pointed and the other rounded. If this strangely shaped egg is pushed, it tends to roll in a circle instead of falling off the ledge.

Each pair of murres on the ledge had its own territory, which was only a few inches wide. A female that was sitting on her egg nearly touched the bird that sat on an egg next to her. The closeness of one bird to another has some advantages, as we have seen. In this case, the birds packed tightly on the windy ledge

A murre perches on a sheer cliff.

The murre's egg is pear-shaped, which helps to keep it from rolling off a narrow ledge.

generated much body heat. It helped to keep both the murres and their eggs warm.

To the man and the woman watching the birds, it seemed almost unbelievable that there should be so much activity on the crowded ledge. The males and females constantly touched each other's bills, and the male nibbled his mate's head. A murre flapped its wings. Another stabbed its bill at a neighbor that had moved too close to its territory. Another bird landed on the ledge, crashing into several birds and almost knocking them over. Then it pushed its way through the crowd and even walked across the backs of other murres to reach its nest.

Much of the noise and activity was caused by young birds that had not found mates. They had not been able to break down their distrust of other birds and form a bond in time to raise a chick that year. Several of these young males clung to a place on the rim of the ledge. They were very interested in the nesting activities going on around them. They often tried to take part. They would go up to a female who was sitting on her egg and nibble her head, or even try to mate with her.

Then there would be an uproar. The mated pair of murres would squawk at the newcomer. They would jab at him with their beaks. Sometimes they would push him right off the ledge, and he would go fluttering down to land on the heads of some startled birds on a ledge below.

Murres are very nervous birds. The young murres on the ledge who did not have mates kept the other murres in an uproar. The nesting birds could be easily frightened. The coming of a boat to the island or the flying of a falcon overhead would create panic among them. The murres would fly off the ledge and land in the water below. Some of them left in such a hurry that they accidentally kicked their eggs off the ledge. The eggs would smash on the rocks at the foot of the cliff.

There was a good reason for the murres being nervous. Herring gulls, standing at the top of the cliff or flying past the ledges, were always watching them. These large white birds are fierce predators of the eggs and chicks of nesting birds. They kept waiting for the murres to leave their eggs unguarded. Then the gulls would fly to the ledge, smash the eggs with their powerful beaks, and gobble the soft insides before the murres returned.

Many of the murres lost their eggs: Some were eaten by gulls. Others were accidentally knocked off the ledges. If a murre lost its first egg, it usually laid another. Watching from the field across the cove, the two ornithologists began to realize how much persistence these birds need to raise a chick on the windswept ledge.

Birds that nest in crowded colonies tend to copy each other's actions. On some ledges, this is an advantage. If the leaders are experienced, the whole colony lays eggs and raises chicks quickly and successfully. On other ledges, some birds are nervous and pass on "the fidgets" to others. Then their eggs are often left unguarded. The gulls eat all the eggs they lay. The unfortunate murres do not raise a single chick in those places.

A Hard Life

A murre's egg is very large. That is because the chick must be well grown by the time it hatches. Birds that are hatched in burrows or stout nests may be naked and helpless at first. But chicks that hatch on the exposed ledge must be able to live in that harsh world.

The murre chick is entirely covered with dark gray fuzz, or down, when it hatches. Its feathers grow quickly. Food does not have to be digested for a chick in the stomach of its parent.

The parents make a great fuss over the chick. One of the parents flies onto the ledge with a small fish called a sand eel. The murre croaks a greeting to its mate. The other bird moves away from the chick it has been guarding and both parents look at it closely, seeming to coo in admiration.

One of the parents forms a broad tent over the chick with its wings. This tent may prevent a neighbor from reaching over and stealing the fish. It also protects the chick, which might become so excited that it will leap at the fish and tumble off the ledge.

The murre chick is not a delicate eater. It seizes the sand eel, which may be longer than itself, and swallows it head first. The chick sometimes begins to digest the head while the end of the tail is still sticking out the side of its beak.

The parent murres display even after the chick has hatched. They bow and rub beaks. One always greets the other when it returns to the ledge. The bond must be kept alive.

The ornithologists across the cove follow the progress of the colony on the cliff not simply by watching it. Sounds and smells reach them even at a distance. The murres are never quiet. The loud cries of the mated pairs fighting off the roaming young males—"Arrgh, arrgh, arrgh!"—"Arr, arr, arr"—comes off the face of the cliff as from a huge sounding board. Dead chicks, rotting eggs, and the droppings of the adults litter the crevices, sending up a powerful stench.

All the parent birds on the ledge are occupied in raising their chicks. Each bird tries to copy the others. An adult that has lost her own egg or chick to the gulls tries to keep up with its neighbors. It brings back fish to the ledge and tries to feed them to the chicks of other murres.

But the other murres pick at the unfortunate bird until it moves away. Then it makes a tent of its own wings. It bows and grunts and slaps the fish on the ledge. It is trying to feed an imaginary chick!

The chicks of murres are as excitable as the adults. When a parent bird jumps up quickly and stumbles all over the chick, the little one fights back. It throws a tantrum. It screeches at its parent so that it sounds like a small gull. It shuffles around on the ledge, still screeching, until the parent soothes it by taking it back under its wing.

The chick is a tough little bird. It lives through long periods of cold rain that often kills the young of other birds. It remains on the open ledge, sitting in wet pools or in filth piled up by all the birds crowded together around it.

After three weeks on the ledge, the chick is nearly ready to leave. It has grown feathers over much of its body. It exercises its wings, flapping them hard as it cries in its tiny voice, "Kwee-wee!"

When the chick is about twenty-five days old, it leaves for the open sea. It makes its way to the rim of the ledge. It beats its wings rapidly and utters its little cries. The cries are answered from other ledges by chicks that are also trying to get up the courage to leap. Sometimes the parent birds stand behind the chick and encourage it too.

At last the chick makes the leap. It steps off the ledge into space. On beating wings that are too weak for true flying, it glides out over the rocks and hits the water with a splash.

A big wave rises over the drifting chick. The little bird knows by instinct how to swim. It dives into the wave just before it breaks and pops up on the other side.

The murre chick is luckier than many other kinds of seabirds. It does not have to make its way out to sea alone. A parent murre has flown down from the cliff to be with it. The adult is waiting for it in the foam on the other side of the wave. Again it calls to the chick with encouragement. The chick paddles in frantic haste to the adult, and they swim together toward the open sea.

The man and the woman have watched this feverish period of seabird life for many weeks. They have written down all that they have seen, and their report will add to what we know about these birds. As they leave, they look once again toward the cliff. Here and there on the ledges are the young murres that did not find mates that year. These birds will be back in another spring. They will feel the urge to find a mate and add their strength to the colony on the open ledge.

9. Gannets and Kittiwakes

Bonaventure Island lies in the Gulf of Saint Lawrence, very close to the coast of the Gaspé Peninsula, in Quebec, Canada. Its shape is round, and it stretches about a mile and a half from one shore to the other. Bonaventure has cliffs too, great reddish walls that rise nearly three hundred feet above the water. On top of the cliffs, the island is covered with grass and spruce trees.

Thousands of people come to see this island every year. They come in small tourist boats from a nearby town on the mainland. Some of the tourists land on the island and walk across the fields to the cliff. Others stay on the boats and look at the cliffs from the sea. They come to watch the birds that nest there: the gannets and the kittiwakes.

Gannets are members of the pelican family. They are the largest and most handsome birds that live in the northern ocean. The kittiwakes are small members of the gull family. These two birds, which often share island cliffs with the murres, have developed other ways to bring up their chicks on the ledges.

Fishermen, who drove the great auks to extinction, went to the islands where gannets nested and killed thousands of them, too. Their colonies were completely destroyed on some islands. But gannets are strong fliers. Unlike the great auks, which could not

The handsome gannet has a six-foot wingspread.

fly, some of the gannets were able to fly away to other islands. They flew to the highest parts of rocky cliffs, where the fishermen and hunters could not reach them. Early in this century, the Canadian Government began to protect them on all the islands where they still nested.

Thousands of gannets nest on Bonaventure Island today. Unfortunately, the gannets are not doing as well on the islands as many people thought they were. But the tourist who comes there sees a huge, colorful colony on a cliff looking like an enormous fortress.

The gannet is a splendid bird. It is about three feet long and weighs about seven pounds. It has fine white plumage with black wing tips and a pointed, gray-blue bill. During the nesting season, the adults grow orange and buff-colored feathers on the head and neck.

The tourists come to Bonaventure to admire the flight of these big birds. The air above the cliffs is filled with gannets flying to

OVERLEAF: *Bonaventure Island, off the coast of Canada, is a favorite nesting site for gannets and kittiwakes.*

and from their nests in the face of the cliff or on the slope above it. The birds often soar in circles over the cliff. They look like drifting crosses in the sky. Their long wings, outstretched, measure six feet from tip to tip. The neck and pointed bill, thrust out before the wings, and the long tail, stretched out behind, complete the form of a cross.

No one who has seen it can ever forget the sight of a gannet that is fishing. The bird flies over the water at a height of anywhere from thirty to a hundred feet. It flies for a few seconds, rapidly beating its wings, then glides with wings spread and motionless. It searches the water below for any sign of its favorite fish: herring and mackerel.

Suddenly the gannet spies a school of mackerel beneath the waves. It tilts and plunges downward at a terrific speed. The bird hits the water with great force and sends up a fountain of spray several feet high. The strong bones of its skull and the small air sacs around its brain protect the bird from injury when it hits the water. The gannet seizes a large mackerel in its bill, swallows it whole, and struggles back into the air.

Some ornithologists like to say that there is no such thing as a "seagull," because gulls usually stay close to land or the islands just off the shore. But this isn't really true. Some gulls go far out to sea. The most seagoing of all the gulls is the little kittiwake, which often flies across the Atlantic Ocean and back. A naturalist who captured one of these birds said that it "refused fresh water and drank salt water eagerly."

Like the gannets, the kittiwakes are very expert fliers. They are named for the high-pitched cry they utter as they circle in flight over a school of fish: "Kittiwake! Kittiwake!" They have white heads and bodies. The tips of their gray wings look "dipped in black ink."

Kittiwakes catch small fish. Sometimes one lands on the water and sticks its head under the surface to seize a fish. At other times it dives like a gannet, dropping from the air and pursuing fish five or six feet underwater. Like auks, kittiwakes are able to use their long wings as fins. They are the only gulls that swim underwater.

The kittiwake sometimes steals building material from its neighbors' nests.

The kittiwake builds a high-walled nest of mud and grass on a narrow ledge.

True Nests and False Teeth

The gannets and the kittiwakes, which are so different in size and appearance, both live comfortably on the cliff's narrow ledges. They solve the problem of caring for their eggs and young on the ledges by building nests like little cribs.

The gannets' nests cover large areas of the cliffs at Bonaventure Island and spill over onto the grassy slopes above. For such large birds, they need very little room. They are packed on the ledges almost as tightly as murres.

The nesting colony is a lively, noisy, smelly place. The birds arrive in the spring and begin to squabble over good nesting sites. When many other kinds of birds fight, they do little harm to each other. But gannets fight savagely. They grasp each other's beak or head in their own beak and wrestle until one of them gives up. These battles do not last very long on the narrow ledges. One bird usually loses its footing and has to start flying quickly before it is dashed on the rocks below.

When gannet pairs select a good nesting territory, they perform a strange courtship dance. They stretch their necks at each other. They bow and raise their wings. They caress each other with their beaks, then tap their beaks together like a couple of fencing masters. They beat their wings and utter harsh, gargling cries: "Urah—rah—rah—rah—rah—rah—rah—rah!"

This display forms the bond between the male and female. Like the male murre, the male gannet is a good husband. The two gannets display for many weeks now as they go about raising a chick together.

The murres prefer to lay their single egg on the bare rock. Gannets build a solid nest for their egg. The male gannet brings seaweed, grass stems, feathers, and whatever else it can find as building materials. Students who have examined gannets' nests have found all sorts of objects built into them: tin cans, a gold watch, and even a set of false teeth.

A British ornithologist, Esther Cullen, has studied kittiwakes and learned how these birds fit themselves for life on the ledges. They build their nests on very narrow ledges or small outcrops of rock that are just a few inches wide. Kittiwakes often do not begin to nest until after a heavy rainfall. Then they are able to find the mud they need in building their nests.

Esther Cullen learned that these little seagoing gulls try to keep from flying over land. Many of the kittiwakes wait on their ledges and watch their neighbors start building their nests. When a neighbor leaves to get more mud or grass, one of the watchers flies to the partly built nest and steals the nesting material. Some kittiwakes return to find that their nests have been pulled completely apart.

Kittiwakes usually take much longer to build their nests than other gulls do. The nest must be solidly built so that it will not blow off the windy cliffs. A kittiwake first collects mud in its long yellow bill. It drops the mud on the ledge and pats it down with its feet to form a solid base for the nest. Then it builds up walls of mud, grass, and seaweed. It lines the inside of the nest with soft grasses. The high walls of this crib will keep the eggs and chicks from rolling out.

Life on the cliffs causes the kittiwakes to behave differently from their gull relatives. Most kinds of gulls are able to tell their chicks from the chicks of their neighbors when they are only a couple of days old. It is several weeks before kittiwakes can recognize their own chicks. Their chicks are not likely to stray from the nest on the narrow ledge. There is no need for their parents to recognize them.

Where Have All the Gannets Gone?

By the middle of summer, eggs are hatching all over the cliffs. Most members of the gull family lay several eggs. Kittiwakes lay two eggs, but usually only one of them hatches. Two lively chicks might cause problems in the little nest that is perched high over the rocks and sea.

The gannet egg is beginning to hatch too. The little bird chips away at the shell with its beak. A crack appears all the way around the shell. The claws on one of the chick's feet show through the crack as it struggles to get out.

A gannet broods its egg.

The shell snaps open at last. The chick tumbles out, as one bird student has said, "helpless, blind, bare as the palm of one's hand, and whining like a puppy dog."

The parents must fly to sea often to dive for fish to feed the young. The gannet that returns to the nest may have trouble in landing. Strong winds sweep the face of the cliff. A sudden gust of wind may throw the big bird against the rocks or the sharp branches of a tree and kill it.

The gannet makes a crash landing in the cramped space around the nest. It has partly digested the fish it caught at sea. It bends over the chick. Now it is easy to see that the gannet is a close relative of the pelican. It opens its beak wide and shows the large throat pouch where it holds the fish.

When the chick is still very young, the parent almost scoops it into the pouch so that it can reach the gooey mass of fish. But the chick grows swiftly, putting on both fat and feathers. After a few weeks, the chick dives right into the roomy throat and pulls out the fish.

The chicks in all the nests prepare to leave the cliffs. They begin to exercise their wings. The kittiwake chick turns to face the cliff when it exercises. Otherwise, a gust of wind might lift it off the ledge and it would find itself hanging out over the sea before it is really ready to fly.

Soon the gannets and the kittiwakes will be at sea. For many years, the cliffs of Bonaventure Island have served as a safe nesting place for seabirds. Thousands of chicks of many kinds have hatched there and flown away to sea. Ornithologists and other people who love birds have come to the island to study them.

The ornithologists who study gannets have made a strange discovery. The cliffs of Bonaventure Island seem to be a safe place to nest, but, every year, fewer gannets nest there.

What has happened to the gannets? Some ornithologists believe that the large numbers of people who come to the island to watch the birds and photograph them are scaring the gannets away. Others believe that pesticides, which are drained from the farms around the Gulf of Saint Lawrence, are killing these birds. Ornithologists will keep on studying the gannets on Bonaventure Island to find out what is happening to them.

The kittiwakes are doing well. Most members of the gull family are more successful than other seabirds today. In the next chapter, we will look at some of these gulls and will see why they are successful and why they are sometimes a menace to other seabirds.

10. Gulls

A LARGE GULL FLEW OVER AN ISLAND where puffins nested. It circled, and then dropped onto a rock. Its pale yellow eyes noticed everything around it. It watched a puffin chick that had wandered too close to the entrance of its burrow. The gull rushed at the chick, seized it in its strong beak, and killed it.

An ornithologist, R. M. Lockley, saw the gull kill the chick. He described what happened next in his book *Puffins:*

"The gull made three attempts to swallow the chick whole. Each time the gull failed it coughed up the body only to pick it up and try again. The gull stretched its throat and its head jerked viciously. After several failures it stood over the body and shrieked angrily. Once more it gulped and failed, choking down black bits of puffin fluff.

"At the next attempt it got the puffin's head down into its throat. It made violent jerks of the head and success seemed near. The meal was half swallowed, the legs and wings still showing, and the gull looked very uncomfortable. Moving a few paces away the gull stretched its neck and swallowed with fierce motions of the bursting gullet. Slowly the bill closed over the last leg and wing.

"The gull was now quite out of shape, the throat bulging in an ivory ball behind the head, which it turned this way and that and

A herring gull searches for food over the North Atlantic Ocean.

gradually pushed the monstrous lunch toward its stomach. Then the gull sat down on a little hill with eyes half closed. Its neck and feathers were puffed up like those of a sick bird."

Lockley went on to describe how the gull finally flew to its own nest and coughed up the dead little puffin. But the gull chicks were not able to tear the puffin apart. The big gull then swallowed the puffin again, after another hard struggle, and walked away. As Lockley wrote: "Evidently supper was not quite prepared yet!"

Visitors to seabird colonies watch gulls attack the chicks of other birds all the time. Gulls are cannibals, too. They eat the chicks of their neighbors if they get a chance. They are hungry predators that stand watch at many large seabird colonies in the northern ocean.

A predator is an animal that kills and eats other animals. The lion that eats a zebra is a predator. So is the robin that eats a worm, or the ladybug that eats an aphid.

OVERLEAF: *Although herring gulls are now very common, they were threatened with extinction in the United States less than a century ago.*

Are predators "bad animals"? Of course not. For thousands of years, human beings gathered the meat they ate by killing weaker animals. Now we raise most of our meat on farms or ranches, but lions, ladybugs, and gulls must hunt for what they eat.

The Ups and Downs of a Herring Gull

The herring gull, which is the most common large gull in the North Atlantic, is a predator on the eggs and chicks of other seabirds. It is also a beautiful and interesting creature. It has existed for thousands of years as a part of the community of wild things in the northern ocean. It captured its share of the eggs and chicks of other birds without threatening them with extinction. This was a natural process, and the other seabirds lived together successfully with the gulls.

But human beings have disturbed the natural process on the ocean, just as they have on land. They have had an effect on all other creatures. Their effect on gulls is one of the strangest stories of all.

At first, it seemed that human beings might wipe out the gulls along the coast of North America. Fishermen and other hunters destroyed all the colonies of great auks. They killed all the gannets, murres, and puffins on many islands. Gulls became very scarce too. In some places, people went to the nesting islands and collected gulls' eggs for food. The gulls lost most of their eggs and raised very few chicks.

Hunters killed thousands of gulls every year for feathers. The feathers of wild birds were very valuable a hundred years ago. Women's hats and dresses were often decorated with the white feathers of gulls. The makers of women's hats paid hunters to go to the islands and kill all the gulls they could find.

People who visit towns and cities in New England today notice gulls everywhere. A hundred years ago, there were few gulls along the coast. An ornithologist who lived in Rhode Island said he did not see a gull for four summers in a row.

Many people were afraid that gulls would become extinct, like the great auks. They formed Audubon societies, which worked

Just out of its shell, this newly hatched herring-gull chick sits beside a pipped egg—the one with the hole in it—from which another chick will soon emerge.

to protect the gulls and other vanishing birds. The government passed laws to protect birds and keep people from taking their eggs and chicks. Around 1900, the gulls began to return.

Some kinds of seabirds have never fully recovered. They are still scarce. But gulls have learned to live alongside people. They have learned to take advantage of the way human beings live and treat the world around them. This is not an accident. To understand the gulls' success, we have to understand something about their way of life.

Will the Real Villain Please Stand Up?

The herring gull is by nature a scavenger. It eats whatever is left lying around: a dead fish, rotting vegetables, garbage of all sorts. It cannot swim underwater like many other seabirds, so it picks up what is floating on the surface, or small fish such as her-

ring that sometimes swim just beneath the surface. On nesting islands, where a gull needs a lot of food for its chicks, it will pick
up whatever is easiest to find. Of course, the easiest things to find
on those crowded islands are the eggs and chicks of other birds.

People became aware of the value of gulls a long time ago.
They realized that gulls were helpful around cities, where the
garbage that piled up or the dead fish that washed ashore often
spread disease. Gulls that came to eat this material were wel-
comed, because they helped to clean up a city.

Sometimes people did not exactly welcome gulls. A farmer in
Massachusetts once bought a load of starfish that fishermen had
brought up in their nets. He wanted to use the starfish as fertil-
izer on his fields. He left the starfish near his house until he
could find time to spread them on the field. When he came for
them, they were gone. The gulls had eaten every one.

What happened to that farmer ought to have been a warning
to people all along the coast. As the human population increased,
so did its garbage. People did not realize that the old ways of
getting rid of garbage did not work anymore, now that there
was so much of it. They went on creating huge garbage dumps
near cities. Farmers left large amounts of unwanted food out in
the open for their pigs and other animals. The owners of fish
canneries dumped all the unwanted parts of the fish back into the
harbor, where they collected in large amounts.

Gulls discovered there was food all around them. They flocked
to the cities and farms and harbors. The numbers of most wild
animals are kept low because of a lack of food. There was no
lack of food for gulls. These scavengers had a population explosion, just as human beings did.

Other seabirds are not so fortunate. Most of them live mainly
on the fish that they catch at sea. Puffins, petrels, gannets, and
terns were not able to learn how to come to the garbage dumps
and fish canneries of human beings. Their populations did not increase. In some cases it was harder than ever for them to find
enough food, because fishermen were taking more fish to satisfy
the growing human population.

There were also fewer places where seabirds could build their nests. People took some of the islands for themselves, and built homes and hotels on them. They allowed destructive animals such as cats, dogs, and rats to get on other islands.

Seabirds retreated to nesting places far offshore. Gulls needed more nesting space too, and they came to those islands in large numbers. During the nesting season, gulls found themselves far from the garbage dumps and other places where they usually fed. Now food was as close to them as the nest of another seabird.

Years ago, the seabirds had been killed on the islands by human beings. Now they faced another danger: They had to try to defend their eggs and chicks against the growing numbers of gulls.

11. Terns

Arctic terns see more of summer, and more of daylight, than any other animal in the world. They breed on islands in the northern ocean, sometimes in the Arctic as far north as they can discover dry land. Then, as autumn arrives, they fly below the equator into Antarctic waters, where they find summer again. They dive for fish there among the floating slabs of ice, under a sky where the sun never sets all summer long.

Now it was May and the terns had come back to the north. Some flocks flew on to the Arctic Circle. Other flocks stayed to nest on islands along the way. One day, fifteen hundred Arctic terns landed on Petit Manan, a small island that lies more than a mile off the coast of Maine.

Petit Manan is a low island. It has no cliffs. It is simply a lumpy field of grass and weeds surrounded by a shoreline of large broken boulders. The only prominent mark on the island is the lighthouse, which is one of the tallest on the Atlantic coast and warns ships away from the rocks.

An Arctic tern stood on one of the big rocks. Terns are among the most beautiful of all seabirds, as anyone who looked at this one for a moment would admit. It was a slender bird, all gleaming white below, with long gray wings and a black cap. Its sharp

The Arctic tern, a graceful long-distance flier, is one of the most beautiful of the seabirds.

bill was bloodred, and so were its legs and feet, which seemed absurdly short.

There are more than thirty kinds of terns in the world. Most of them nest in warmer regions. Three kinds—the Arctic tern, the common tern, and the roseate tern—had been coming to nest on Petit Manan for a number of years. They looked almost exactly alike, except that the Arctic tern had a redder bill, and its legs were a little shorter, than the others.

The Arctic tern flew off the rock and out over the water. It was a light and graceful flier, rising and falling on strong wing-beats and easily changing course. Suddenly it rose a little higher, its bill pointed straight downward, and seemed to stop in midair. Then it folded its wings and dove head first into the water.

This slender bird did not make a big splash, like a gannet, nor did it disappear from view. It hit the water with a little *splat!* and flew back up into the air a second later with a small silver fish hanging from its red bill. The tern shivered its wings to flick off the water drops and then turned toward the island. As it flew, it uttered a series of high-pitched cries. Anyone watching might have expected the tern to open its mouth wide and lose its fish when it made such a loud cry. But the tern screeched with its mouth tightly closed. It seemed to be telling the world that it had caught a fish.

People who live along the coast often call the terns "sea swallows" because of their long, pointed wings and forked tails. It was this beautiful plumage that almost caused the terns to disappear. Like the gulls, their close relatives, they were hunted everywhere for their feathers. During the nineteenth century, fashionably dressed women had their hats decorated with the feathers and even the entire bodies of terns.

Laws were passed just in time to save these beautiful creatures. But terns eat only the fish they catch. They don't eat the great variety of foods that gulls do, and so they were not able to take advantage of mankind's garbage. They have not been able to fit into the modern world the way gulls have, and they face many dangers today.

No one suspected that Arctic terns were such remarkable birds. Then, in the 1920s, an ornithologist named Oliver L. Austin, Jr., banded many of these birds in Labrador. Some of them were found thousands of miles away with the bands still on their legs. One of the chicks that Austin banded in Labrador was found three months later in South Africa. These studies proved that Arctic terns fly farther in migration than any other birds in the world. Some of them travel more than twenty-two thousand miles every year.

Perhaps even more amazing is the fact that these birds, which fly so many miles over the ocean, are poor swimmers. Their legs are too small and weak to serve as good paddles. If they cannot find a beach or an island where they can set down for a rest, they usually land on a floating piece of wood. A scientist once put some terns in a tank of water that had no resting place. The terns paddled for a little while and then drowned.

Terns make a simple nest on the bare ground or rock.

The Gift

A few days after the Arctic terns land at Petit Manan, one of them carries a small fish back to the island. It screams loudly and begins to chase another tern. The other tern flies in front of it, its neck stretched out strangely before it. It is a sign that the terns are starting their courtship.

After that, all the male terns display to the females. They make spectacular flights over the island, gliding and diving. The males and females of terns, like many other seabirds, look exactly alike. When another bird comes into a male tern's territory on the island, he pecks at it. If the other bird fights back, he knows the bird is a male. But if the bird turns its bill away, he knows a female has come and wants to be friendly.

Terns do not build much of a nest. They simply scrape away a little dirt or sand or find a dent on a rock. If there happen to be some twigs and plant stems nearby, they will sprinkle them around the nest, but they will not fly any distance to find them.

The female lays her eggs in this nest. She usually lays two, but some terns lay one, three, or even four eggs. Both parents incubate them. Like many other seabirds, their displays go on right through the breeding season.

The display between two Arctic terns is a very pretty sight. The male flies in from the sea with a little fish in his bill. He struts across the rock near the nest. His mate ignores him at first. He circles her, dangling the fish. She keeps on turning away.

The male tern refuses to be ignored. Finally his mate faces him and accepts his "gift." The proud male stretches his neck toward the sky and calls. He steps lightly over the rock as if he were doing a little victory dance.

Petit Manan is as noisy as other islands during the nesting season. Terns are especially nervous, noisy birds. They are always moving around, uttering their shrill cries. If a person walks onto the island near their nests, all the birds immediately fly up into the air. They screech at the visitor—"Kak, kak, kak!"—as they dive at his head. Ornithologists who study tern colonies wear thick caps or even hard hats, because terns strike so fiercely that they can draw blood from the scalp.

One of the strangest sights at a tern colony is a "panic flight." Everything will be quiet on the island. No person or predator will appear to startle the birds. But suddenly, for some reason that no one can explain, all the birds will spring into the air— thousands of them at once—in absolute silence. They will fly madly around for a minute or so. Then, setting up their cries again, they will return to their rests.

A Sad Story

Late in June, the eggs begin to hatch. A chick pecks its way out of the egg and crawls into the nearby grass. It is covered with brownish fluff spotted in black. The fluff is wet and matted for a short time; then it dries and the chick becomes a lively little creature that is able to run into the grass and hide if danger appears when its parents are away from the nest.

A chick is never really safe at Petit Manan. One morning, a large gull flies low over the island. The terns fly up into the air, diving and screaming at the invader. The gull ignores the mob of

A tern chick has just been fed by its parents, and is begging for food.

terns that swirls around it. It dips low in its flight and seizes a downy tern chick in its bill. Beating its large wings, it gets back up into the air, its feathers flying as the angry terns peck savagely at its back. As the gull flies away, it swallows the chick with one enormous gulp.

The terns of all kinds that nest on Petit Manan may lay three thousand eggs or more in a summer. Most of those eggs will hatch, but very few of the chicks will leave the island alive. There are many things that can go wrong.

Every year, some tern chicks die of disease. Others die when human beings come on the island and frighten the adult terns from their nests. If the sun is very strong that day, the chicks may become overheated and die before their parents return to shelter them. Hundreds of chicks die of the cold and dampness during long periods of rain on northern islands.

Chicks starve on the island when they are not fed regularly. The only food that the terns know how to eat are herring and other small fish they catch at sea. Sometimes, especially in bad weather, these fish do not stay near the surface and are hard to find. When terns fly back from the sea without fish, the young birds will suffer.

Terns have always faced such problems. In years when disasters struck them, they raised very few young. But, the following year, the weather might be good and many hundreds of chicks would grow in the nests and fly off to sea at the end of summer. The terns are fitted by nature for life in the northern ocean.

But things are different today. There is a small island next to Petit Manan called Green Island. The island is green, of course, because nesting seabirds—especially gulls—have fertilized it with droppings for years. At one time, only a few gulls nested there. But now there is plenty of food at fish canneries and garbage dumps on the coast of Maine.

The gulls have had a population explosion. Large numbers of herring gulls nest on Green Island. Great black-backed gulls, which are fierce predators, too, also began to nest on Green Island when food became plentiful. Jeremy Hatch, an ornithologist who studied the terns on Petit Manan for several years, often watched gulls fly from Green Island to capture tern chicks. He reports that the gulls may eat between seven hundred and fifty and fifteen hundred chicks a year on the island.

This is the sad story of terns along most of the Atlantic coast. As the gulls increase, they reach more of the islands where terns used to nest in safety. The nervous terns finally give up and try to find new places to nest.

In many cases, gulls have forced the terns to move to poor nesting places. They have pushed the terns to the edges of islands, where storms and high tides wash away their nests. They have pushed the terns to islands too close to the mainland, where they cannot find enough food for their young. Other predators, such as foxes, rats, and owls, easily reach those islands and kill terns and their chicks.

Ornithologists have tried to help the terns on some islands. They have tried to drive the gulls away, but there are so many gulls that it is very difficult. The men and women who care about seabirds are using their skill and imagination to find new ways to help them.

12. A Suitcase Full of Puffins

A SUITCASE FULL OF PUFFINS sounds as far out as a taxi full of elephants. Why would anyone put puffins in a suitcase? That's what the man was carrying, however, and there was a very good reason for the trip.

Stephen J. Kress is a young ornithologist. He likes to watch seabirds, especially puffins, and he wishes that there were more of them along the Atlantic coast of the United States. Puffins nested on some of the islands near Maine years ago, but fishermen killed them for food or bait. Finally, only one American island had any puffins left.

Steve Kress decided to try to put puffins back on one of the islands where they used to nest. If the plan worked, there would be more puffins along the Maine coast. If the plan did not work, scientists would still learn a great deal about puffins. He selected an island named Egg Rock, where the last puffins were killed about eighty years before.

The Canadian Government allowed Kress to land on an island near Newfoundland where thousands of puffins nested. They knew that he was a careful scientist who would do everything he could to protect the birds he took. Kress and his helpers gathered one hundred chicks from burrows on the island and took them to Maine.

71

A baby puffin is a ball of frizzy black down.

That was why Steve Kress was carrying a suitcase full of puffins. He had made five large wooden cases and covered one side of each of them with cloth so that the birds were able to breathe. He fastened twenty large round juice cans, with their lids off, in each case. A juice can, lying on its side in the case, was just large enough to hold a puffin chick.

It was a fast trip. Kress and his helpers picked up the chicks in the morning and then went by boat and truck to an airport in Newfoundland. They flew to Maine, where another truck was waiting for them.

"We didn't feed the chicks on the trip, because we didn't want them to soil their juice cans," he said. "I did bring an ice chest full of small frozen fish with me. I was afraid we might have bad weather and the plane would be grounded. I'd have felt pretty silly sitting around in a motel room for a couple of days with a hundred hungry puffin chicks!"

The truck rushed Kress and the chicks to a dock on the Maine coast. There a boat was waiting to take them to Egg Rock, six miles out at sea. It was almost midnight by then. There was a light fog on the water as the boat traveled down the bay.

"We've built a burrow on the island for each of the chicks,"

Kress said. "We dug up the ground into burrows that are the same size and shape that these chicks came from in New-foundland. Then we put the sods of earth back over the bur-rows. Each of the burrows has an entrance, a tunnel, and a nest-ing chamber. Then we'll cover the entrance with wire so the puffins cannot get out until they're large enough to leave the is-land on their own."

Puffin Village

The boat reached the island and Kress took the cases of puffins ashore. Egg Rock is like many other small Atlantic islands. There are no trees growing on it. A field of weeds and grasses grows in the middle, surrounded by a large jumble of rocks sloping down to the water. Some gulls nested on the island. Kress put wire over the entrances to the burrows to keep the gulls out as well as to keep the puffins in.

The light from lanterns hollowed out the darkness around a large clearing in the grass where the burrows were prepared. It looked like a little village. There were paths that crisscrossed the area, dividing the colony into small "blocks." There was a wooden sign with a number on it in front of each burrow so that Kress could keep track of the chicks.

He opened one of the cases. Twenty tiny, dark-colored crea-tures squatted in their juice-can "burrows" and stared out at the lanterns. Kress pulled a chick from one of the cans and held it up to the light. It was about ten days old. It was covered with long, blackish-brown down that looked almost like silky fur. It had a white patch on its belly and a broad, gray beak. The chick uttered faint peeping noises. It was hard to believe that this shapeless ball of dark fluff would someday grow into a colorful puffin, as a homely caterpillar blossoms into a lovely butterfly.

"Isn't it a tough little bird?" Steve Kress asked as he stroked the chick. "Bounced around in boats, trucks, a plane, no food all day, and now some nosy people pulling it out of bed at mid-night! It's got a right to be pretty upset."

He lowered the chick into a burrow. As the chick scrambled

A puffin fledgling has left its burrow and is finding its way across the island to the sea.

down the tunnel, Kress spread a handful of small silver fish called smelts in the burrow and fastened a square piece of chicken wire over the entrance. Then he put the other chicks in their own burrows.

"We'll bring a big ice chest full of smelts out here to the island and feed the chicks three times a day," Kress explained. "We'll even put some vitamin pills inside the smelts' mouths once in a while to make sure the chicks get a healthy diet."

Steve Kress had no idea how his plan would work out, but he hoped it would start puffins nesting on the island again in a few years. He knew it would not be possible to bring adult puffins to Egg Rock and make them stay there to nest. Ornithologists know, however, that seabirds usually return to nest on the islands where they were raised. He took these chicks from their parents as young as possible. Puffin chicks need to have the warmth of a brooding parent for the first week of their lives. Kress hoped that these chicks would regard Egg Rock as their home and be attracted back to it when they became adult puffins and were ready to breed.

It took the chicks more than a month to become strong

A young puffin exercises its wings.

enough to leave the island. Kress and the students who helped
him put up a big tent on the island so they could remain near the
chicks. They planted lettuce and tomatoes to go with the peanut
butter, jam, and cereal they brought with them, and the fish and
lobsters they bought from passing fishermen.

Kress had built four of the burrows with plexiglass roofs so
that he could watch the chicks during the day. The chicks led a
lazy life, moving around mostly at feeding time. Sometimes they
poked the ground or the walls of the tunnel with their stout bills
or picked up stems of grass and held them for a few moments.
As they grew older and feathers began to push out the down, the
chicks exercised their wings in the dark burrow.

Outward Bound

When the chicks were six weeks old they were ready to leave
the island.

"We take away the wire every night now," Kress said. "The
chicks like to come out about midnight and walk around a little
and exercise their wings. Then they go back in. We think the

puffin somehow gets to know the island on these brief walks, and that might be enough to get it to come back here and nest some-day."

He reached into a burrow and pulled out a chick. It kicked energetically. It was a far different creature from the one Kress had brought to the island. The body was well covered with feathers, and the white belly patch had spread over most of the chest. Steve Kress looked at the bird proudly.

"Two of the chicks died since we brought them here, but the other ninety-eight are all strong and healthy," he said. "They weigh more than most chicks do at their natural nesting colonies. That extra fat could be important for their first few days at sea, when they are learning to fish for themselves."

Kress put a colored band on a leg of each bird so that he would be able to recognize it if it ever came back to Egg Rock. Then he waited for the puffins to leave. He knew that even on the islands where the chicks are raised by their parents they will leave the burrow one night by themselves and make their way to sea.

It was after midnight, and a faint moon hung in the sky. Steve Kress was sitting on a rock near the burrows. Suddenly a chick walked past him. It stumbled and fell between two rocks but immediately climbed out and walked on. A chick protected by its fat and feathers is seldom hurt even on a long fall to the rocks. The chick beat its wings to help it over the next crevice in the rocks. Then it reached the sea and swam off into the dark.

It may be five years before a puffin is old enough to breed. But Steve Kress hopes that someday he and other people who love seabirds will see a nesting colony on Egg Rock once more.

13. Ripples on the Sea

FAR TO THE NORTH of Egg Rock there is another, larger island. It lies where icy currents mingle in the northern ocean. Thousands of puffins breed there every summer. The chicks are not treated so carefully, even by their parents, as the ones taken by Steve Kress. Gulls swoop in and kill them. Sometimes a parent brings a fish that is much too large back to the burrow and the chick chokes to death on it. Or the parents cannot find enough food in stormy weather and the chick starves.

Yet the island is a delight to anyone who loves seabirds. The birds live here in the numbers and variety that make a seabird colony one of the grandest sights on earth. There are movement and color, and smells and noise. The visitors who watch the colony catch the feverish excitement and they feel more alive themselves.

An adult puffin comes out of a burrow and scrambles up the face of a steep rock, beating its wings to keep its balance. It stands on the rocks and looks with great curiosity at the puffins that are walking around in their bowlegged way on the rocks nearby. No one can look at a puffin without wanting to take its picture. It is a fantastic-looking creature, certainly one of the wonders of the bird world.

A puffin scrambles up the steep side of a rock.

The puffin is an auk. It is a relative of the murres, razorbills, and the extinct great auks. As the visitor watches the puffins bustle around on the rocks and poke their noses into every other puffin's business, they begin to seem almost human and look much larger than they really are.

The adult puffin stands about a foot tall. During the long winter at sea it is a rather plain, black-and-white bird like the other auks. Now, during the nesting season, the adult takes on all sorts of colorful touches. The back and wings remain black, but the feathers on the bird's face, chest, and belly become a more sparkling white. Black feathers cover the back of its head and form a collar around the throat. Its webbed feet are a bright red. A writer once described the bird this way:

"The puffin looks like a rich old man in a dinner suit, complete with black jacket, white shirt front, black bow tie, and a very red nose."

It is this "nose" that receives so much notice, both from human beings and from the other puffins. The beak, which is smaller and not very colorful during the winter, grows a set of horny plates and ridges in the summer. It is shaped like a heart lying on its side. The base of this beak runs from the forehead all

During the summer, the puffin's large beak becomes a brilliant red, gold, and blue.

the way to the chin. It is colored partly a bright, fire-engine red. The rest is a kind of bluish gray and pale gold. A wrinkled clump of orange flesh separates the bill from the puffin's face.

There is a great deal of activity on the rocks. One of the puffins opens its beak wide and displays the bright yellow lining. Another puffin lowers its head to peer into a burrow. The owner of the burrow rushes out angrily to chase the inquisitive bird away. A fight starts. The two birds grab each other's beak and twist this way and that. The fight attracts a crowd of puffins, which rush up to see what is happening. The two birds quickly settle down, but the others wander aimlessly about on the spot, as if talking over what they have seen or hoping that something else will happen.

A puffin enters its burrow.

Puffins are continually flying in from the sea. They beat their stubby wings rapidly and roll from side to side in flight, so that at one moment they show the white feathers of the belly and the next moment the black feathers of the back. A puffin comes in for a landing on the rock where the fight took place. It spreads its tail to help slow it down and extends its bright red feet like airplane landing gear. It lands with a bump, staggers a bit, then folds its wings and stands upright on the rock.

The puffin's huge beak is crammed with fish. There are at least eight small fish, their heads and tails drooping over the edges of the beak like a silvery mustache. People wonder how a puffin, swimming underwater, can open its mouth to catch that last fish without losing all the others. Scientists say that the puffin kills a fish with one crunch of its powerful beak. Then, with its tongue, it pushes the fish to the rear of the beak, where sharp little sawlike points on the beak hold the fish in place. The puffin is able to keep opening its mouth without losing the fish it has already pushed to the rear.

The puffin looks carefully around to make sure there are no gulls or other enemies in sight. Then it runs down the slope of a rock, the fish dangling from its beak, and disappears into its burrow. There it drops the fish on the ground for the chick.

The other parent has been sitting with the chick. Now it leaves the burrow. It flies quickly across the rocks and lands in the water, where it immediately begins to bathe. The bird floats on one side and then on the other, beating its wings so that the water falls on it like a shower. The puffin rolls in the water,

A puffin can hold many fish in its beak.

OVERLEAF: *Seabirds are spread out all over the world for most of the year, coming together only during the nesting season.*

ruffles its feathers, and finally flaps its wings. It rests for a while, smoothing the loose feathers to make them water-resistant. At last the bird flies away to sea in search of fish.

Back in the puffinry, which is what a puffin colony is sometimes called, the bustle goes on. Puffins threaten each other with their big beaks or stand around in little groups. They are mostly quiet, but once in a while a bird roars in its burrow and a sound like the motor of a chain saw rises from the entrance. It is a reminder that life goes on under the rocks as well as on top of them.

The drama that a visitor sees there on the island has been taking place in the northern ocean for hundreds of centuries. During that vast expanse of time, the puffins, storm petrels, murres, gannets, terns, kittiwakes, and other seabirds have developed the displays, fishing skills, and nesting habits that fit them for life in that harsh world.

In recent centuries, that way of life has been threatened. Millions of seabirds are killed every year when they are caught in oil spills from tankers or trapped in the nets of fishermen. They are driven off their nesting islands by mammals brought there by human beings, or by gulls whose population grows because of the waste provided by modern civilization.

Each nesting island, no matter how far it is from the great cities on the coasts, is tied in some way to what goes on in those cities. Despite its great size and the storms that sweep across it, the North Atlantic is like a little pond where the ripples set in motion by a falling pebble travel to its farthest corners. The oil spill that occurs on a distant coast may wipe out the puffins that have been nesting for years on an island thousands of miles away.

For much of the year, the birds are spread out over the sea, facing its many dangers. It is only in the nesting season that they come together on the islands in all their numbers and marvelous variety. People of all ages, and from all over the world, travel to see these colonies. We know now that seabirds are as much a part of the ocean as the whales and the seals, the schools of herring, and the great cliffs that rise out of the fogs.

Index

ADA AND FRANK GRAHAM have long been active in the fields of ecology and conservation. They live on the coast of Maine, where Mrs. Graham has developed a series of nature programs for children and Mr. Graham is a field editor for *Audubon*, the magazine of the National Audubon Society. Together they have written many books for young readers, including a series of "Audubon Readers," THE MYSTERY OF THE EVERGLADES, PUFFIN ISLAND, THE CARELESS ANIMAL, and MILKWEED AND ITS WORLD OF ANIMALS, which was awarded a Children's Science Book Award by the New York Academy of Sciences. Mr. Graham is also the author of the highly acclaimed SINCE SILENT SPRING and MAN'S DOMINION: THE STORY OF CONSERVATION IN AMERICA.

LES LINE is editor of *Audubon* magazine and a well-known nature photographer who has collaborated with the Grahams on several books for young readers. He has spent many weeks photographing seabirds on their breeding islands from Canada and Maine to Alaska. Among his many books are SEASONS, THE SEA HAS WINGS, THIS GOOD EARTH, THE PLEASURE OF BIRDS, THE AUDUBON SOCIETY BOOK OF WILD BIRDS, and THE AUDUBON SOCIETY BOOK OF WILD ANIMALS. His wife, Lois, and his children, Heather and Michael, accompanied him on the expeditions that produced many of the pictures in this book.